P9-CLP-394

Sequoyah

SPIRIT
of America®

Sequoyah

NATIVE AMERICAN SCHOLAR

By C. Ann Fitterer

The
Child's
World

The Child's World®
Chanhassen, Minnesota

8

Sequoyah

Published in the United States of America by The Child's World®
PO Box 326 • Chanhassen, MN 55317-0326 • 800-599-READ • www.childsworld.com

Acknowledgments

The Child's World®: Mary Berendes, Publishing Director

Editorial Directions, Inc.: E. Russell Primm, Emily Dolbear, and Lucia Raatma, Editors; Linda S. Koutris, Photo Selector; Dawn Friedman, Photo Research; Red Line Editorial, Fact Research; Irene Keller, Copy Editor; Tim Griffin/IndexServ, Indexer; Chad Rubel, Proofreader

Photos

Cover: Raymond Gehman/Corbis; National Portrait Gallery, Smithsonian Institution/Art Resource, NY: 6; Private Collection/Bridgeman Art Library: 17; Raymond Gehman/Corbis: 2, 9; David Muench/Corbis: 7; Kevin Fleming/Corbis: 11; Sally A. Morgan;Ecoscene/Corbis: 21; Danny Lehman/Corbis: 26 top; Annie Griffiths Belt/Corbis: 26 bottom; Georgia Historical Society, Savannah, Georgia: 23; Hulton Archive/Getty Images: 19; Library of Congress: 13, 14, 24, 25, 27; North Wind Picture Archives: 8, 15, 20; Stock Montage: 10; Western History Collections, University of Oklahoma Libraries: 22; Woolaroc Museum, Bantlesville, OK: 28.

Library of Congress Cataloging-in-Publication Data

Fitterer, C. Ann.
Sequoyah : Native American scholar / by C. Ann Fitterer.
    p. cm.
Includes bibliographical references.
Summary: A brief introduction to the life of the Cherokee Indian who created a method for his people to write and read their own language.
ISBN 1-56766-167-X (Library Bound : alk. paper)
1. Sequoyah, 1770?–1843—Juvenile literature. 2. Cherokee Indians—Biography—Juvenile literature.
[1. Sequoyah, 1770?-1843. 2. Cherokee Indians—Biography. 3. Indians of North America—Biography.]
I. Title.
E99.C5 S3826 2003
975.044'9755'092—dc21

2001007400

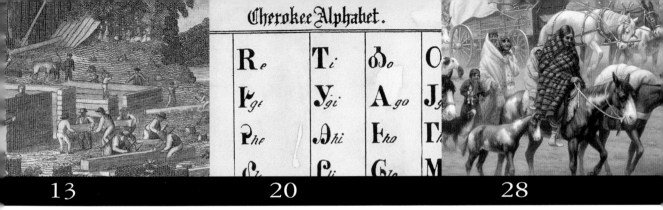

13 20 28

Contents

Chapter ONE

Part Indian, Part White

THE MOST FAMOUS CHEROKEE INDIAN IN history was named Sequoyah (sih-KWOY-uh). His life was often difficult, but he didn't let that keep him from his dream. Almost 200 years ago, he gave his people the gift of reading and writing their own Cherokee language.

Because Native Americans did not keep written records, no one knows exactly when Sequoyah was born. It is believed that he was born in 1770 in a Cherokee village in the

A portrait of Sequoyah

Smoky Mountains of what is now Tennessee. Sequoyah's Cherokee name was Sogwali. **Missionaries** gave him the name Sequoyah later in his life. He is sometimes called Sequoya.

Sequoyah's mother was an important woman from a noble Cherokee family. Her name was Wuh-teh. Her family knew many things about the history of the Cherokee people. Because the Native Americans did not have a written language, they counted on people to remember and share the stories of their past.

Sequoyah was born in the Smoky Mountains of Tennessee.

Historians believe that Sequoyah's father was a white trader named Nathaniel Gist. Gist married Wuh-teh and lived with her in

7

Nathaniel Gist, shown here next to George Washington during the French and Indian War, was probably Sequoyah's father.

the Cherokee village. Sadly, Gist left his family when Sequoyah was a baby and never returned.

Sequoyah grew up without a father and had no brothers or sisters. It was not easy to be part Indian and part white in the Native American culture. Some Cherokee people did not respect him.

Although Sequoyah loved to play with the other boys in the village, he had a hard time fitting in. Because of a disease—or perhaps a hunting accident—one of his legs did not work properly. The leg ached and made it hard to run.

Sequoyah was a shy and quiet boy. He often went to the woods to draw instead of playing with the other children. He liked to draw the animals of the forest.

As a teenager, Sequoyah's artistic skill showed in other ways, too. He made things out of wood. Sometimes he used silver to make beautiful jewelry. Sequoyah started to travel from village to village, selling what he had made. People got to know him.

In one village, Sequoyah became interested in the work of a **blacksmith**. He studied with the blacksmith until he learned that skill too.

Like these Cherokee tour guides at the Cherokee Indian Reservation in North Carolina, Sequoyah carved things out of wood.

ABOUT 400 YEARS AGO, THE CHEROKEE INDIANS LIVED IN THE EASTERN United States. They lived in what are now the states of Tennessee, North Carolina, South Carolina, Virginia, West Virginia, Kentucky, Georgia, Alabama, and Arkansas (see map below from about 1900). Over many years, as the white settlers moved to America and built homes, the Cherokee were forced to leave this large area. They moved to parts of North Carolina and Oklahoma.

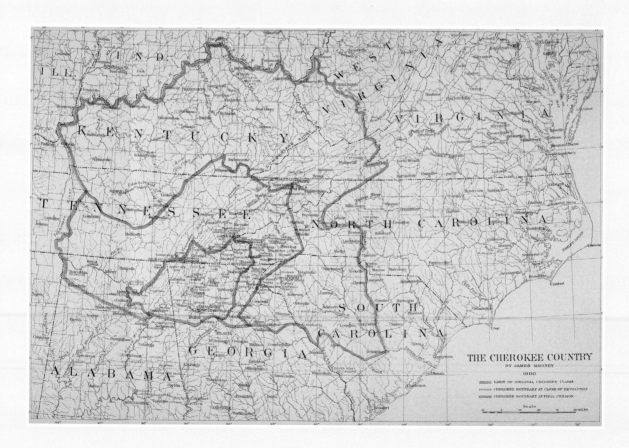

THE CHEROKEE COUNTRY
BY JAMES MOONEY
1900

The Cherokee Indians built their homes in a cluster. The **council house** stood in the center. The leaders of the tribe met in this building. The Cherokee huts were usually round. The wooden walls were covered with mud and grass. The roof was made of bark.

The Cherokee were skilled hunters and fishers. They also grew plants in fields and gardens for food.

The Cherokee enjoyed feasts, songs, and dances. They had songs for many of their everyday tasks as well as for important occasions.

Today, many Cherokee Indians still live in Oklahoma and North Carolina. At special festivals, they dress in ceremonial clothing (above). Today, the Cherokee people are the largest Native American group in the United States. Their government is called the Cherokee Nation.

Chapter TWO

"Talking Leaves"

SEQUOYAH DECIDED TO END HIS TRAVELS. He met a Cherokee woman named Utiya and settled down.

The couple lived in a house in a village called Willstown. Sequoyah worked as a blacksmith in the village and also made silver jewelry. His work was well known and respected. Utiya and Sequoyah had four sons. They also had a baby daughter named Ah-yoka. Life was very good for Sequoyah.

Over time, however, Sequoyah became upset by the fact that white settlers were moving onto land that the Native Americans had lived on for centuries. Not only were the Native Americans losing their homes, but they were also giving up their traditions. Some of them were even adopting the settlers' way of life.

Interesting Fact

▶ Sequoyah's English name is George Guess. The name "Guess" is believed to be a misspelling of "Gist," which was his father's last name.

Sequoyah was sad to see these changes. As a child, he had learned the wonderful stories of the Cherokee people from his mother. The Cherokee way of life was very important to him. He was sad to see it slowly changing.

During Sequoyah's lifetime, many white settlers moved onto Indian land.

In 1812, the American people fought the British. Some Cherokee Indians decided to help the Americans fight their battles. The Cherokee thought that the Americans might reward them by giving back the land they had taken. Sequoyah decided to join the many other Cherokee Indians who served with the U.S. Army in the War of 1812.

In that war, Sequoyah made new friends. One of them was a chief named John Ross. Like Sequoyah, John Ross was part Cherokee and part white. Unlike Sequoyah, John had been raised in the whites' way of life and had been sent to school. He could speak Cherokee, and he could also read and write English.

One day, Sequoyah was with John Ross and some white soldiers when a bag of mail arrived. Sequoyah watched the men as they read their "talking letters." He was fascinated.

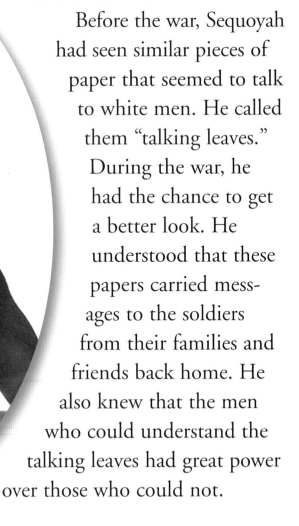

Cherokee chief John Ross was Sequoyah's friend.

Before the war, Sequoyah had seen similar pieces of paper that seemed to talk to white men. He called them "talking leaves." During the war, he had the chance to get a better look. He understood that these papers carried messages to the soldiers from their families and friends back home. He also knew that the men who could understand the talking leaves had great power over those who could not.

John Ross explained to Sequoyah how the written English language worked. He explained how some people had learned to read the language.

Sequoyah thought about this idea for a long time. He wondered if it would be

During the war, Sequoyah recognized the value of words on paper.

possible to read the Cherokee language. Finding a way to communicate in the Cherokee language with these talking leaves would be important to his people, he realized.

15

Chapter THREE

Inventing a Syllabary

ALMOST TWO YEARS AFTER HE JOINED THE soldiers, Sequoyah returned home to his family. By now, his sons were grown. His baby daughter Ah-yoka was a young girl. Once again, he made his silver jewelry and worked in his blacksmith shop.

Sequoyah's work no longer interested him as it had in the past, however. He could not stop thinking about the talking leaves. Sequoyah decided to make a written language. He started drawing pictures on pieces of bark for all the Cherokee words.

He worked all day long on his pictures. He worked day after day. He no longer worked with silver. He didn't go to the blacksmith shop either. His sons did all the work in the fields. His collection of pictures grew and grew.

16

Sequoyah's friends in the village began to worry about him. They didn't understand what he was doing. They thought his behavior was very strange. Even Sequoyah's wife and sons did not understand his pictures. But Ah-yoka spent many hours with Sequoyah while he worked.

Sequoyah drew thousands of pictures to represent Cherokee words. Some words were difficult to express in a picture. He struggled to figure out how to deal with all the words. He had to think of more and more **symbols**.

Sequoyah devoted himself to creating a written language for his people.

Sequoyah's friends and family grew impatient with him. The people of the village began to joke about him. One day, Utiya could no longer control her frustration with her husband. She took his collection of pictures and threw them into their fire. Now his work was ashes.

But still Sequoyah would not give up his

work. He was determined to find a way to record the Cherokee language. In fact, he had already decided on a new approach. Instead of trying to create a picture for every Cherokee word, he would provide a written symbol for every sound, or **syllable**. That way, one symbol could be used for many words. He set to work again.

Life was no longer happy for Sequoyah, however. He no longer had the respect of his family or the village people. They all thought he was crazy. He decided to leave the village and took Ah-yoka with him. They traveled far to the West to live with Cherokee people who had not heard the unkind stories about him.

On their way, Sequoyah met a woman named Sally, who was traveling with her son—Squirrel Boy. They became good friends. By the time they reached the Arkansas Territory, where they planned to settle, Sequoyah and Sally decided to marry.

Sequoyah built a house for his new family. He also set up a trading post. Sally encouraged him to continue his work with the written language. Life was once again good for Sequoyah.

18

He spent months and months listening to people talk. He recorded each sound and gave it a symbol. Sometimes he didn't need as many symbols as he had thought because two sounds turned out to be the same. Many symbols were letters from an English spelling book he had seen a few years before. He changed some letters and made up new symbols.

After years of hard work, Sequoyah had identified 86 syllables. Because the symbols represented syllables instead of letters, he had invented a **syllabary**, not an alphabet.

In Arkansas, Sequoyah and his new family set up a trading post like the one shown here.

Now it was time to see if Sequoyah's writing system worked. Ah-yoka already knew the signs from the time she had spent with Sequoyah. They taught the symbols to Sally and Squirrel Boy. They learned quickly. It was almost like a game. The family learned to talk to each other using the "talking leaves."

An early example of Sequoyah's syllabary

Sequoyah could not believe his dream had come true! After 12 years, he had created a great gift for his people. Now Sequoyah had to deliver his gift to the leaders of the Cherokee people.

Cherokee Alphabet.

D $_a$	R $_e$	T $_i$	δ $_o$	O $_u$	i $_v$
S $_{ga}$ O $_{ka}$	F $_{ge}$	Y $_{gi}$	A $_{go}$	J $_{gu}$	E $_{gv}$
θ $_{ha}$	P $_{he}$	θ $_{hi}$	F $_{ho}$	Γ $_{hu}$	ɸ $_{hv}$
W $_{la}$	σ $_{le}$	P $_{li}$	G $_{lo}$	M $_{lu}$	ɸ $_{lv}$
ɸ $_{ma}$	O1 $_{me}$	H $_{mi}$	ʃ $_{mo}$	Y $_{mu}$	
Θ $_{na}$ t $_{hna}$ G $_{nah}$	Λ $_{ne}$	h $_{ni}$	Z $_{no}$	ɸ $_{nu}$	O $_{nv}$
T $_{qua}$	ω $_{que}$	P $_{qui}$	V $_{quo}$	ω $_{quu}$	ε $_{quv}$
U $_{sa}$ ωs $_{s}$	4 $_{se}$	b $_{si}$	ɸ $_{so}$	ɸ $_{su}$	R $_{sv}$
L $_{da}$ W $_{ta}$	S $_{de}$ ɸ $_{te}$	Λdi ɸti	V $_{do}$	S $_{du}$	ɸ $_{dv}$
δ $_{dla}$ L $_{tla}$	L $_{tle}$	C $_{tli}$	ɸ $_{tlo}$	ɸ $_{tlu}$	P $_{tlv}$
G $_{tsa}$	V $_{tse}$	Ir $_{tsi}$	K $_{tso}$	d $_{tsu}$	C $_{tsv}$
G $_{wa}$	ω $_{we}$	Θ $_{wi}$	ω $_{wo}$	θ $_{wu}$	6 $_{wv}$
ω $_{ya}$	B $_{ye}$	ʃ $_{yi}$	f $_{yo}$	G $_{yu}$	B $_{yv}$

20

IN CALIFORNIA, HUGE redwood trees tower over the land below. These are the tallest and oldest trees in America. In 1847, Austrian scientist Stephen Endlicher gave this great trees the name *Sequoia sempervirens*. Historians believe Endlicher named the tree after Sequoyah as a tribute to the Cherokee Indian.

The United States has also remembered Sequoyah by naming a national park after him. In 1890, land in California's Sierra Nevada was set aside to protect the sequoia trees growing there (above). The Sequoia National Park is the second-oldest park in the United States.

Just south of the Sequoia National Park is the Sequoia National Forest. This beautiful woodland, established in 1908, also honors the great Cherokee Indian named Sequoyah.

Chapter FOUR

A Beloved Old Man

Sequoyah working with his daughter Ah-yoka on his writing system.

IT WAS 1821. SEQUOYAH DECIDED TO TAKE Ah-yoka with him to meet with the Cherokee Tribal Council. They traveled all the way from the Arkansas Territory to the state of Georgia. John Ross, Sequoyah's friend from the War of 1812, was the leader of the council.

Sequoyah presented his syllabary to the council. At first, the chiefs did not believe him. Sequoyah told the group that he and his daughter would show them how it worked.

After Sequoyah left the building, the chiefs gave Ah-yoka a message. She wrote the correct symbols down. Sequoyah returned, looked at the symbols, and spoke the exact message the chiefs had given. Then, the chiefs ordered Ah-yoka to leave the building and gave Sequoyah a message to record. Ah-yoka returned and studied what Sequoyah had written. She read the message exactly as the chiefs had said it. The chiefs were stunned. Sequoyah and his daughter could talk on paper!

Soon, young and old Indians were coming to Sequoyah to learn the written language. The Cherokee people learned quickly. They wrote with—and on—whatever they could find.

After a year of teaching the Cherokee in the east, Sequoyah and his daughter traveled west to their home. Along the way, they taught Cherokee people how to communicate by writing. Soon, the Cherokee were sending each other letters.

Within a few years, parts of the Bible were translated into Cherokee. In 1828,

A printed page of the Bible in the Cherokee language

Samuel Austin Worcester started publishing the Cherokee Phoenix *in 1828.*

Sequoyah and a missionary named Samuel Austin Worcester published the first copy of a Cherokee newspaper. It was called the *Cherokee Phoenix*.

Sequoyah would take no payment for the years of work spent developing and then teaching his syllabary. But the leaders of the Cherokee Nation knew what a wonderful gift Sequoyah had given them. They decided to give him money every year for the work he had done. In 1824, they presented him with a beautiful silver medal and gave him the title of Adviser of the Nation. Sequoyah became one of several important leaders whom the Cherokee people considered "Beloved Old Men."

By this time, more white settlers had moved onto Cherokee land. President Andrew Jackson used the U.S. Army to force the Cherokee to leave their lands. In 1828, the Cherokee, including Sequoyah, were forced to move far to the west, to what is now Oklahoma. Because thousands of

ᏣᎳᎩ **ᏗᎰᎱᎦᎵ** (Cherokee syllabary masthead)

CHEROKEE PHOENIX.

VOL. I.   NEW ECHOTA, THURSDAY APRIL 10, 1828.   NO. 8.

The front page of the Cherokee Phoenix *from April 10, 1828*

Cherokee died before it was over, this journey was called the Trail of Tears.

By now, it was 1842 and Sequoyah was about 70 years old. He thought back to the stories his mother had told him about the first Cherokee people. She told him that his **ancestors** had come from Mexico. He decided to travel there. He also wanted to see if the language in Mexico was similar to the

The inside of Sequoyah's home in Oklahoma as it looks today

This fast-food menu in Tulsa, Oklahoma, is written in English and Cherokee.

Cherokee language. He thought he might try to create a syllabary for the Mexican language.

Sequoyah left for Mexico along with his oldest son and three other men. Sally stayed in Oklahoma with Ah-yoka, who was now married and had children. A year after he left Oklahoma, Sequoyah died near a Mexican village called San Fernando.

Sequoyah's work allowed his people to communicate with one another and write down their history. Sequoyah will always be remembered for giving the Cherokee their own written language.

Visitors to the U.S. Capitol in Washington, D.C., can see this statue of Sequoyah, which was a gift from Oklahoma after becoming the 46th state.

AS MORE AND MORE WHITE SETTLERS MOVED TO THE EASTERN UNITED States, they took over more land for their farms. In 1830, the U.S. government passed laws that forced the Native Americans to give up their land and move west, away from the white settlements.

The Native Americans refused to move. The U.S. Supreme Court supported the Indians. It ruled that the government could not make them leave their land. But the U.S. Army moved in and removed all the Native Americans from this part of the eastern United States anyway.

The soldiers treated the Cherokee like animals. They rounded up almost 17,000 Native Americans and forced them to walk for months (below). They headed to what is now the state of Oklahoma. They had to walk in the coldest part of the winter and into the spring. When summer came, it was very, very hot.

Thousands of Native Americans died on this dreadful trip. This sad part of American history is known as the Trail of Tears.

c. 1770 Sequoyah is born in a Cherokee village in the Smoky Mountains of what is now Tennessee. His mother is Cherokee and his father is most likely a white trader named Nathaniel Gist.

1813–1814 Sequoyah serves with the U.S. Army in the War of 1812 and the Creek War, a battle that took place during the War of 1812.

1821 Sequoyah completes his syllabary of the Cherokee language. He and his daughter Ah-yoka travel to Georgia to present the syllabary to the Cherokee Tribal Council.

1824 Sequoyah receives a silver medal from the Cherokee Nation for giving his people a written Cherokee language.

1828 Sequoyah and a missionary named Samuel Austin Worcester publish the first copy of the Cherokee newspaper called the *Cherokee Phoenix*. It is the first Native American newspaper in history.

1838–1839 The U.S. Army forces some 17,000 Cherokee, including Sequoyah, to move far west to what is now Oklahoma. Thousands of Cherokee died during the Trail of Tears.

1842 Sequoyah travels to Mexico with his son and three other men to look for Cherokee people and perhaps create a syllabary for the Mexican language.

1843 Sequoyah dies near a Mexican village called San Fernando.

1847 An Austrian scientist named Stephen Endlicher names the huge redwood trees of California after the great Cherokee scholar Sequoyah.

1908 The Sequoia National Forest is established in honor of Sequoyah.

ancestors (AN-sess-turz)
Ancestors are family members who lived long ago. Sequoyah's mother told her son that their ancestors came from Mexico.

blacksmith (BLAK-smith)
A blacksmith makes horseshoes and repairs iron tools. Sequoyah worked as a blacksmith for a while.

council house (KOUN-suhl HOWSS)
A council house is the meeting place for the tribal leaders who make important decisions for the group. Cherokee Indian leaders met in a council house.

missionaries (MISH-uh-nayr-eez)
Missionaries are people sent by a church to teach others about their religion. Missionaries gave Sequoyah his name.

phoenix (FEE-niks)
A phoenix is a legendary bird said to have lived 500 or many thousands of years ago. In 1828, Sequoyah and missionary Samuel Austin Worcester published the *Cherokee Phoenix*. It was the first Cherokee newspaper and the first Native American newspaper.

syllabary (SIL-uh-bayr-ee)
A syllabary is a table of symbols that represent syllables instead of letters. Sequoyah invented his syllabary of the Cherokee language after years of hard work.

syllable (SIL-uh-buhl)
A syllable is a unit of sound in a word. The word syllable has three syllables. Sequoyah identified 86 syllables in the Cherokee language.

symbols (SIM-buhlz)
A symbol is something that stands for something else. Sequoyah created a written symbol for every syllable in the Cherokee language.

For Further INFORMATION

Web Sites

Visit our homepage for lots of links about Sequoyah:
http://www.childsworld.com/links.html

Note to Parents, Teachers, and Librarians:
We routinely verify our Web links to make sure they're safe,
active sites—so encourage your readers to check them out!

Books

Cwiklik, Robert. *Sequoyah and the Cherokee Alphabet.* Morristown, N.J.:
Silver Burdett Press, 1980.

Klausner, Janet, and Duane H. King. *Sequoyah's Gift: A Portrait of the
Cherokee Leader.* New York: HarperCollins Children's Books, 1999.

Oppenheim, Joanne. *Sequoyah, Cherokee Hero.* Mahwah, N.J.: Troll
Communications, 1980.

Roop, Peter, and Connie Roop. *Ahyoka and the Talking Leaves.* New York:
HarperCollins Children's Books, 1992.

Places to Visit or Contact

Sequoyah Birthplace Museum
To find out about visiting Tennessee's only Indian-operated historical attraction
576 Highway 360, Citico Road
Vonore, TN 37885
423-884-6246

Museum of the Cherokee Indian
*To see original material in the Cherokee syllabary and thousands of rare
photographs and books*
P.O. Box 1599
Cherokee, NC 28719
828-497-3481

Index